100 FACTS
Mummies

100 FACTS
Mummies

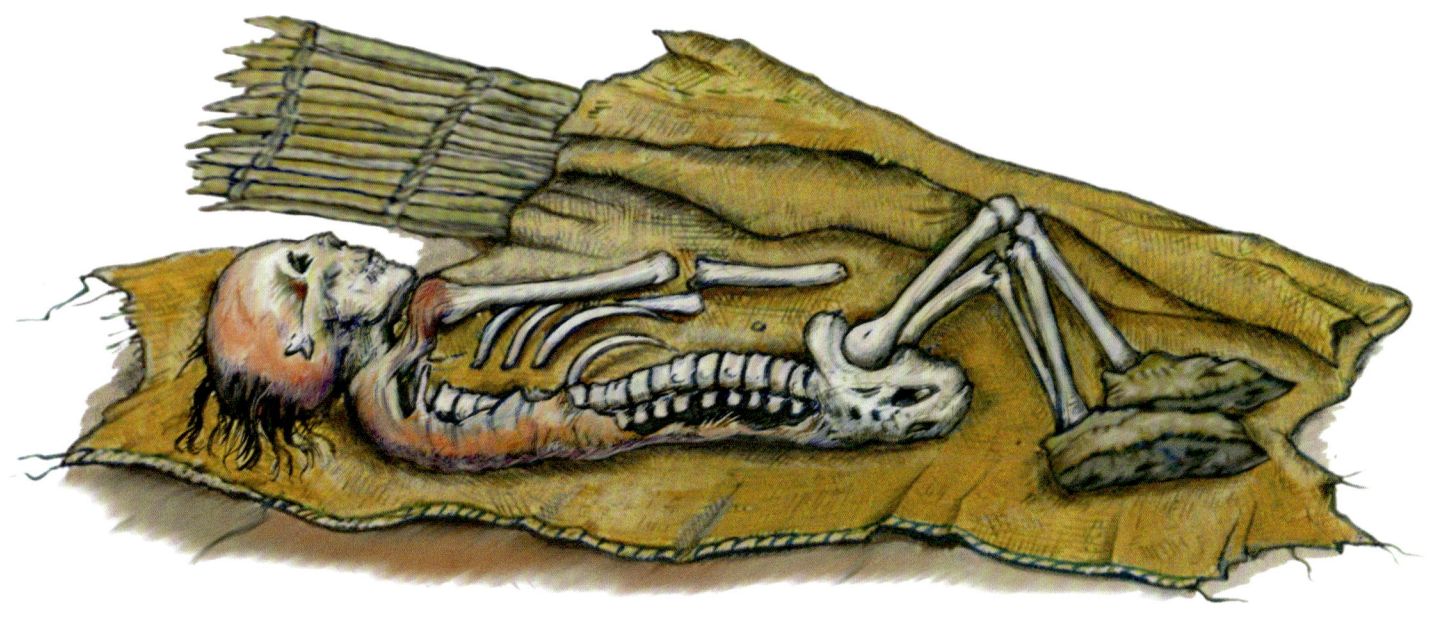

John Malam
Consultant: Fiona MacDonald

Miles Kelly

First published in 2007 by Miles Kelly Publishing Ltd
Harding's Barn, Bardfield End Green, Thaxted, Essex, CM6 3PX

Copyright © Miles Kelly Publishing Ltd 2007

This edition printed 2022

10 12 14 13 11

Publishing Director Belinda Gallagher
Creative Director Jo Cowan
Editorial Director Rosie Neave
Editorial Assistant Carly Blake
Volume Designer Sally Lace
Image Manager Liberty Newton
Indexer Hilary Bird
Production Jennifer Brunwin
Reprographics Stephan Davis
Assets Lorraine King

All rights reserved. No part of this publication may be reproduced, stored in a retrieval system, or transmitted by any means, electronic, mechanical, photocopying, recording or otherwise, without the prior permission of the copyright holder.

ISBN 978-1-78989-583-4

Printed in China

British Library Cataloguing-in-Publication Data
A catalogue record for this book is available from the British Library

ACKNOWLEDGEMENTS
The publishers would like to thank the following artists who have contributed to this book:
Mike Foster, Andrea Morandi, Mike Saunders
All other artwork from the Miles Kelly Artwork Bank

The publishers would like to thank the following sources for the use of their photographs:
Key: t = top, b = bottom, c = centre, l = left, r = right
Cover Christophe Boisvieux/Corbis NX/Getty
Alamy 14(b) World History Archive **Diomedia** 44(b) DeAgostini/Dea Picture Library
Fotolia 24(bg) fotolia.com **John Malam** 43(cr) **Getty** 12(b) Christophe Boisvieux/Corbis NX;
13(tl) Christina Gascoigne/robertharding; 40(b) AFP **Movie Store Collection** 45(cl) Karl Freund/Universal Pictures
Topfoto 16-17(tc) & 28(tl) Heritage-Images; 29(tl), 32(tr) & 38(tr) 2003 Credit:Topham Picturepoint;
38(b) & 41(tr) Charles Walker; 39(cl) 2004 Fortean/Trottmann; 41(b) Roger-Viollet; 42(bl) John Massey Stewart;
43(bl) Fortean; 45(tr) Universal Pictures, Alphaville Films, Imhotep Productions/2001 Credit:Topham Picturepoint;
46-47(tc) Sputnik; 47(b) PA Photos **Werner Forman Archive** 36(br)

All other images from the Miles Kelly Archives

Every effort has been made to acknowledge the source and copyright holder of each picture.
Miles Kelly Publishing apologizes for any unintentional errors or omissions.

Made with paper from a sustainable forest

www.mileskelly.net

Contents

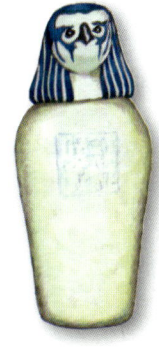

What is a mummy? 6

The first mummies 8

Iceman of Europe 10

Bog bodies 12

Lindow Man 14

Mummies of ancient Egypt 16

Egypt's first mummy 18

A very messy job 20

Drying the body 22

Wrapped from head to toe 24

Tombs and tomb robbers 26

Tutankhamun, the boy-king 28

Magnificent mummies! 30

Mummies of Peru 32

Mummies from Asia 34

North American mummies 36

Worldwide mummies 38

Studying mummies 40

Animal mummies 42

Mummy stories 44

Modern-day mummies 46

Index 48

What is a mummy?

1 **A mummy is a dead body that has not rotted away.** Natural mummies are accidents of nature, made by freezing, drying or waterlogging. Artificial mummies are made on purpose, by people who have used different ways to preserve bodies. The best known artificial mummies were made in ancient Egypt. Long ago, travellers from Persia (modern-day Iran) thought that a sticky black substance, called bitumen, was used to make Egyptian mummies. The Persian word for bitumen was *mummia*, and from this comes the English word 'mummy'.

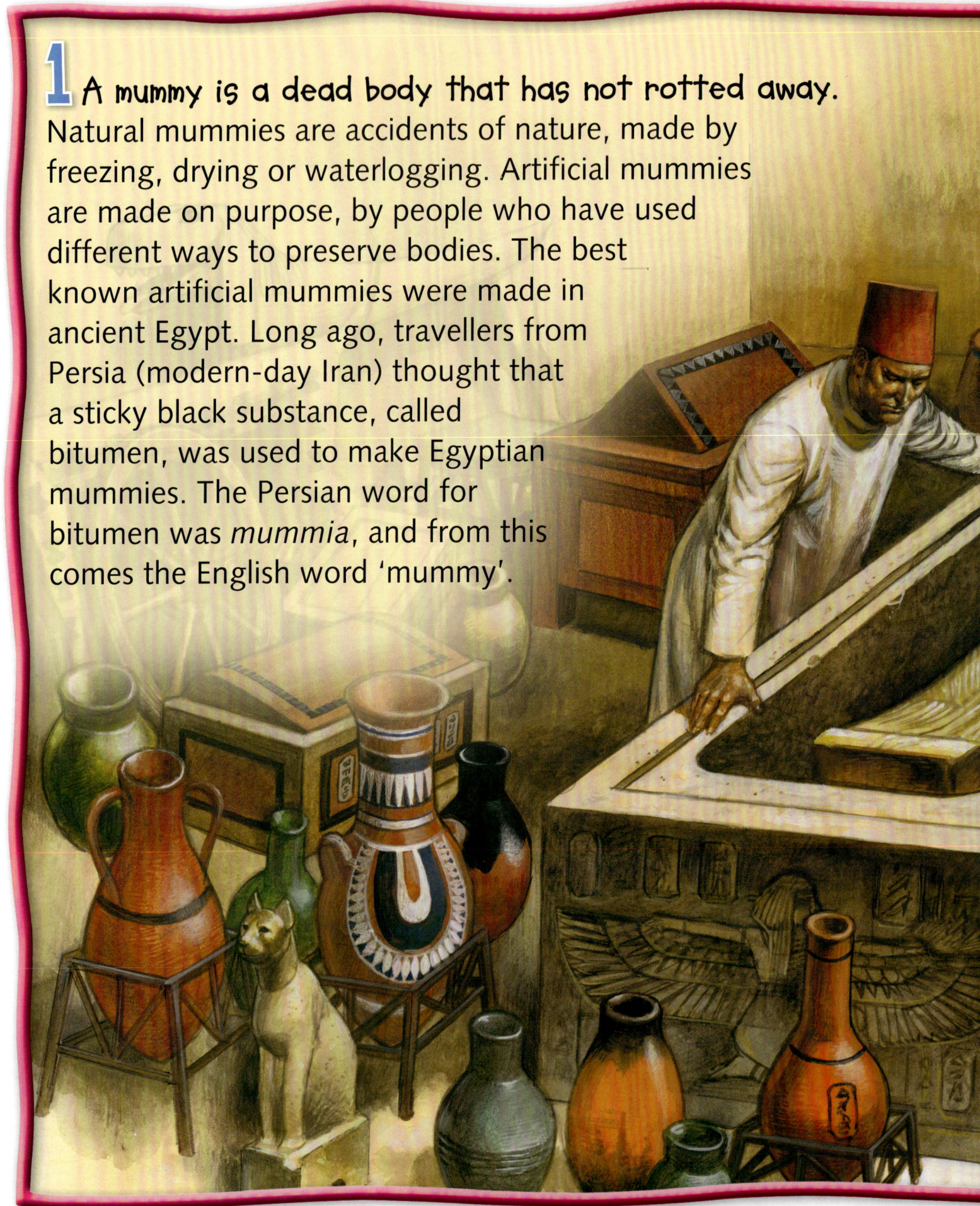

▲ The 3300-year-old mummy of Egyptian pharaoh Tutankhamun was discovered in 1922 by Howard Carter. This is a good example of an artificial mummy.

The first mummies

2 The first artificial mummies were made 7000 years ago by the Chinchorro people of South America. These people are named after a place in Chile. Here, scientists discovered traces of the way the Chinchorro lived. They were a fishing people who lived in small groups along the coast of the Pacific Ocean.

QUIZ

1. Where did the Chinchorro people live?
2. What was put on a mummy to make a body shape?
3. For how many years did the Chinchorro make mummies?
4. When were the first mummies discovered?

Answers:
1. Chile in South America 2. White mud 3. 3000 years 4. 1917

▼ A clay mask was sometimes placed over the face of a Chinchorro mummy.

3 It is thought that the Chinchorro made mummies because they believed in life after death. They tried to make a mummy look as lifelike as possible, which shows they did not want the person's body to rot away. Perhaps they thought the dead could live again if their bodies were preserved.

4 To make a mummy, the Chinchorro first removed all of a dead person's insides. The skin and flesh were then taken off the bones, which were left to dry. Then sticks were tied to the arm, leg and spine bones to hold them together. White mud was spread over the skeleton to build a body shape. The face skin was put back in place, and patches of skin were added to the body. When the mud was dry, it was painted black or red.

◀ Once the Chinchorro had removed all the skin and soft tissue, the body was rebuilt with sticks, mud and paint.

5 The Chinchorro made mummies for about 3000 years. Early mummies were painted black, but by the time of the last mummies, 4000 years ago, the Chinchorro were painting them red.

6 The first Chinchorro mummies were discovered in 1917, when 12 were found buried in northern Chile. In 1983, builders uncovered more of this ancient burial ground. About 100 ancient Chinchorro mummies were dug up at this site, and more have been found elsewhere in Chile.

Iceman of Europe

7 Europe's oldest human mummy is known as the Iceman. He died about 5300 years ago, at the end of the Stone Age. His mummy was discovered by hikers in northern Italy in 1991. They found it lying face down in an icy glacier.

8 The Iceman mummy was found high up in the mountains, where it is very cold. At first, people thought that he was a shepherd, or a hunter on the search for food – or even a traveller on a journey. Then in 2001, an arrowhead was found in the Iceman's left shoulder. He might have fled into the mountains to escape danger.

9 When the Iceman was alive, arrows had sharp points made from flint (a type of stone). It was a flint arrowhead that injured the Iceman, piercing his clothes and entering his left shoulder. This arrow caused a deep wound. The Iceman pulled the long arrow shaft out, but the arrowhead remained inside his body. This injury would have made the Iceman weak, eventually causing him to die.

◀ The Iceman is the oldest complete human mummy ever to be found. He is so well preserved, even his eyes are still visible.

10 The mummy's clothes were also preserved by the ice. For the first time, scientists saw how a Stone Age person actually dressed. The Iceman wore leggings and shoes made from leather, a goatskin coat, a bearskin hat and a cape made from woven grass. These would have kept the Iceman warm in the cold climate.

11 **Equipment used by the Iceman was also found with him.** He carried a copper axe, a flint dagger, and a bow and quiver with 14 arrows. He also had a leather pouch filled with dried grass, which he would have used for starting fires. If the Iceman had been a hunter, he would have killed animals, such as the mountain ibex (a type of goat), with his arrows.

12 **Today, the Iceman mummy and his clothes and equipment are kept at a museum in northern Italy.** Visitors are able to peep through a tiny window to see the Iceman, who is kept frozen inside a special room. The mummy must never be allowed to thaw, as this would cause it to rot.

▶ This reconstruction of the Iceman shows how he would have looked on the day he died.

I DON'T BELIEVE IT!
At first, the Iceman was thought to be a modern person who had died in a recent accident on the mountain.

Quiver to hold arrows

Leather pouch

Flint dagger

Copper axe

Shoes stuffed with grass for warmth

Bog bodies

I DON'T BELIEVE IT!
When Tollund Man was found, scientists could only save his head. His body was left to dry until only the bones were left.

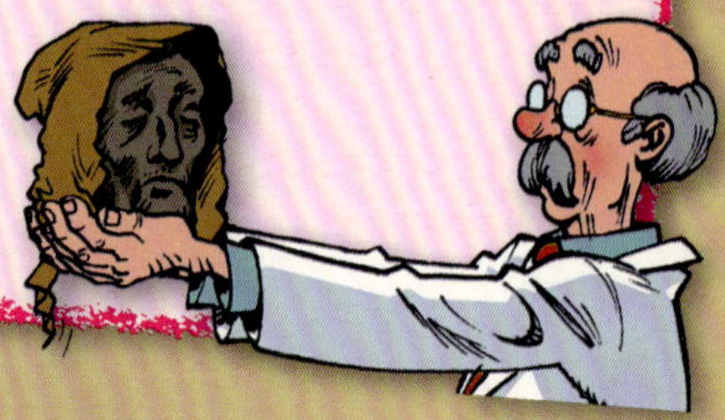

13 Lots of mummies have been found in the peat bogs of northern Europe. Peat is a soily substance that is formed from plants that have fallen into pools of water. The plants sink to the bottom and are slowly turned into peat. If a dead body is placed in a bog, it may be preserved as a mummy. This is because there is little oxygen or bacteria to rot the body.

14 Bog bodies, or mummies, are usually found when peat is dug up. One of the best known bodies was dug up at Tollund, Denmark, in 1950. Tollund Man, as he is known, died 2300 years ago. Around his neck was a leather noose. He was hanged, perhaps as a sacrifice to his gods, and then thrown in the bog. Over the years his face was perfectly preserved, right down to the whiskers on his chin.

▶ The face of Tollund Man is so well preserved, he looks as if he is sleeping.

15 **Grauballe Man was also found in a peat bog in Denmark.** He was discovered by peat workers near the village of Grauballe in 1852. About 2300 years ago, the man's throat was cut and he bled to death. His body was thrown into a bog, where it was preserved until its discovery.

▲ The head of Grauballe Man. Like all bog bodies, his skin has turned brown due to the acids in the bog.

16 **Bog bodies have also been discovered in Germany.** At Windeby, the body of a teenage girl was found. The girl, who died 1900 years ago, was wearing a blindfold. It seems she was taken to the bog, her eyes were covered, and then she was drowned. A heavy rock and branches were put on top of her body, so it sank to the bottom of the bog.

▶ The mummy of Windeby Girl revealed that some of her hair had been cut off, or shaved, at the time of her death.

17 **From the Netherlands comes the bog body of another teenage girl.** Known as Yde (*ay-de*) Girl, she was stabbed, strangled and then dumped in a bog around 1900 years ago. A medical artist made a copy of her skull, then covered it with wax to rebuild her face. The model shows scientists how Yde Girl may have looked when she was alive.

Lindow Man

18 A bog body of a man was found in north-west England in 1984. It was discovered by peat cutters at Lindow Moss, Cheshire. The mummy was named 'Lindow Man', but a local newspaper nicknamed it 'Pete Marsh' because a peat bog is a wet, marshy place. Lindow Man is now on display at the British Museum, London.

19 Lindow Man was about 20 years old when he died. His short life came to an end around 1900 years ago. After his death, his body was put in a bog, where it sank without trace until its discovery by the peat cutters.

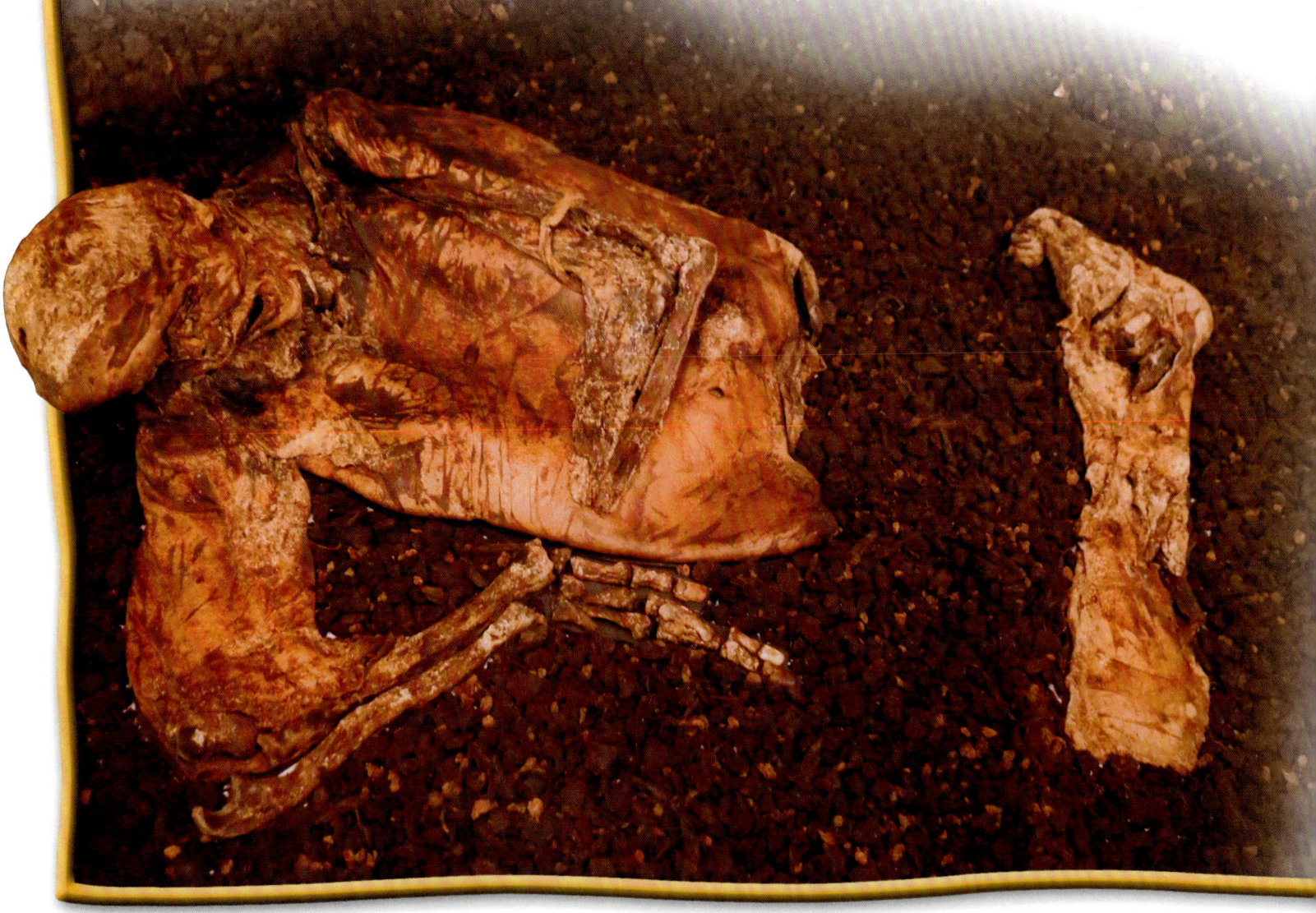

▼ The body of Lindow Man was squashed flat by the weight of the peat on top of it.

20 **Lindow Man did not die peacefully.** Before he died, he ate food with poisonous mistletoe in it. It's impossible to say if the poison was put there on purpose, or by accident. The marks on his body tell the story of his last moments alive. Someone hit him hard on the head, a cord was tightened around his neck and he was strangled. Then, to make sure he was dead, his throat was cut.

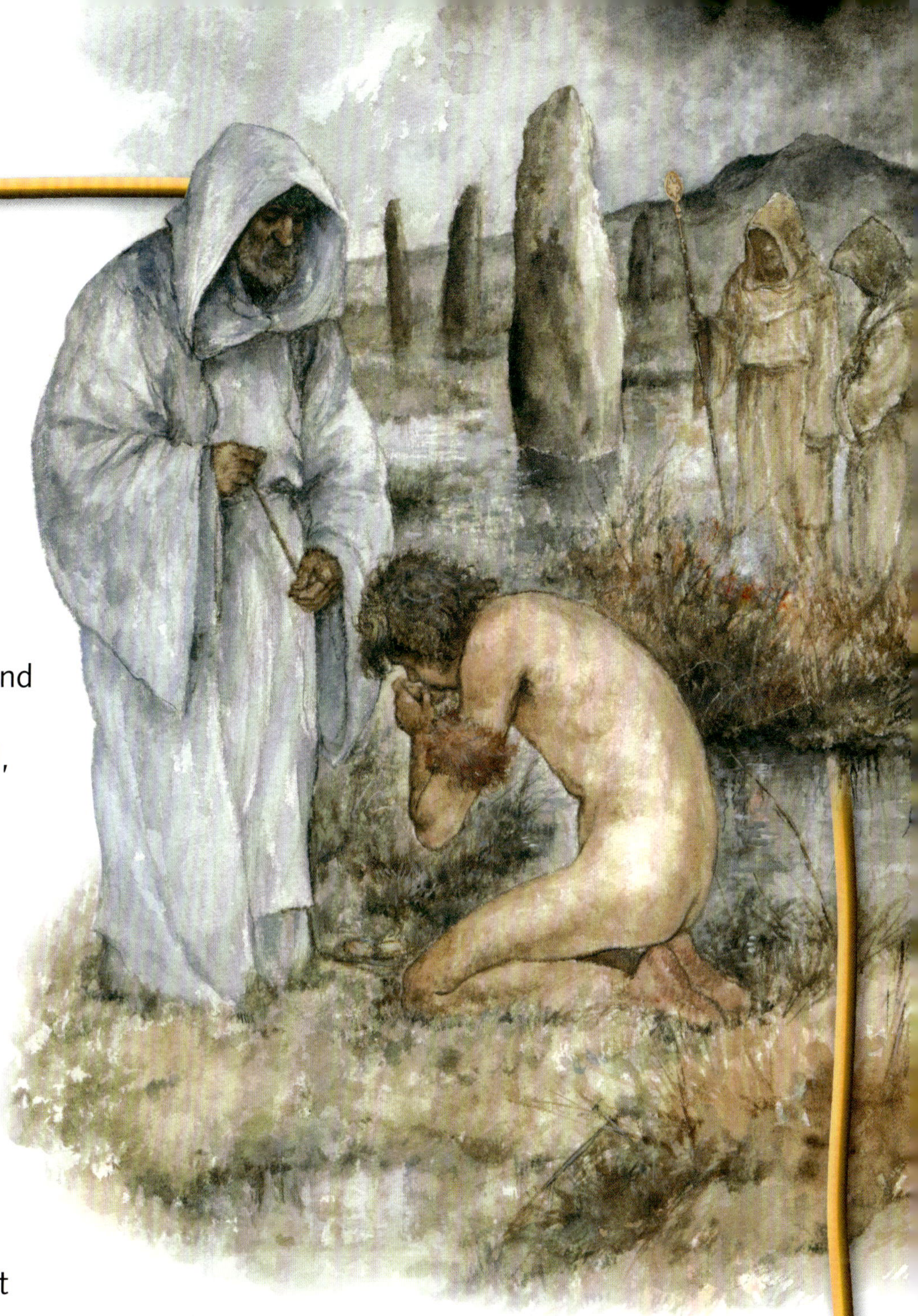

21 **It took four years to find most of Lindow Man's body.** The machine used to cut the peat had sliced it into pieces, which were found at different times. His top half, from the waist up, was found in 1984, and four years later his left leg turned up. His right leg is missing, possibly still buried in the peat bog.

▲ In this reconstruction, Lindow Man eats a meal containing burnt bread. This may have been part of a ceremony in which he was sacrificed to the gods.

I DON'T BELIEVE IT!
Visitors to the British Museum have come up with names for Lindow Man, including Sludge Man and Man in the Toilet!

22 **In Lindow Man's time, gifts were given to the gods.** The greatest gift was a human sacrifice, which is what may have happened to Lindow Man. After eating a meal mixed with mistletoe, he was killed and put in a bog. People may have thought he was leaving this world and entering the world of the gods.

15

Mummies of ancient Egypt

23 The most famous mummies were made in ancient Egypt. The Egyptians were skilled embalmers (mummy-makers). Pharaohs (rulers of Egypt) and ordinary people were made into mummies, along with many kinds of animal.

▲ Even pet dogs were mummified in ancient Egypt.

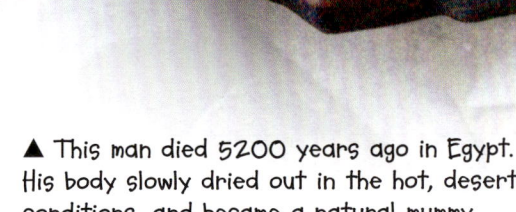

▲ This man died 5200 years ago in Egypt. His body slowly dried out in the hot, desert conditions, and became a natural mummy.

▲ Two people walk through the Field of Reeds, which was the ancient Egyptian name for paradise.

24 Mummies were made because the Egyptians thought that the dead needed their bodies in a new life after death. They believed a person would live forever in paradise, but only if their body was saved. Every Egyptian wanted to travel to paradise after death. This is why they went to such trouble to preserve the bodies of the dead.

25 Ancient Egypt's first mummies were made by nature. When a person died, their body was buried in a pit in the desert sand. The person was buried with objects to use in the next life. Because the sand was hot and dry, the flesh did not rot. Instead, the flesh and skin dried and shrivelled until they were stretched over the bones. The body had been mummified. Egypt's natural mummies date from around 3500 BC.

26 The ancient Egyptians made their first artificial mummies around 3400 BC. The last mummies were made around AD 400. This means the Egyptians were making mummies for 4000 years! They stopped making them because as the Christian religion spread to Egypt, mummy-making came to be seen as a pagan (non-Christian) practice.

27 When an old grave was found, perhaps by robbers who wanted to steal the grave goods, they got a surprise. Instead of digging up a skeleton, they uncovered a dried-up body that still looked like a person! This might have started the ancient Egyptians thinking – could they find a way to preserve bodies themselves?

▶ Many Egyptian coffins were shaped like a person and beautifully painted and decorated.

Egypt's first mummy

28 The ancient Egyptians told a myth about how the very first mummy was made. The story was about Osiris, who was ruler of Egypt. It explained how Osiris became the first mummy, and because it had happened to him, people wanted to follow his example and be mummified when they died.

29 The story begins with the murder of Osiris. He had a wicked brother called Seth, and one day Seth tricked Osiris into lying inside a box. The box was really a coffin. Seth shut the lid and threw the coffin into the river Nile, and Osiris drowned. Seth killed his brother because he was jealous of him – he felt the people of Egypt did not love him as much as they loved Osiris.

30 Isis was married to Osiris, and she could not bear to be parted from him. She searched throughout Egypt for his body, and when she found it, she brought it home. Isis knew that Seth would be angry if he found out what she had done, and so she hid the dead body of Osiris.

▶ Isis, Anubis and Thoth rebuild the body of Osiris to make the first mummy.

QUIZ

1. Who killed Osiris?
2. Who was the wife of Osiris?
3. How many pieces did Seth cut Osiris into?
4. Which three gods helped Isis?
5. What did Osiris become in the afterlife?

Answers:
1. Seth 2. Isis 3. 14 4. Ra, Anubis, Thoth 5. King of the dead

31 However, Seth found out, and he took the body of Osiris from its hiding place. Seth cut Osiris into 14 pieces, which he scattered far and wide across Egypt. At last, he thought, he had finally got rid of Osiris.

32 Seth might have destroyed Osiris, but he could not destroy the love that Isis had for him. Once again, Isis searched for Osiris. She turned herself into a kite (a bird of prey), and flew high above Egypt so she could look down upon the land to see where Seth had hidden the body parts of Osiris. One by one, Isis found the pieces of her husband's body, except for one, which was eaten by a fish.

33 Isis brought the pieces together. She wept at the sight of her husband's body. When Ra, the sun god, saw her tears, he sent the gods Anubis and Thoth to help her. Anubis wrapped the pieces of Osiris' body in cloth. Then Isis, Anubis and Thoth laid them out in the shape of Osiris and wrapped the whole body. The first mummy had been made. Isis kissed the mummy and Osiris was reborn, not to live in this world, but to live forever in the afterlife as the king of the dead.

A very messy job

34 Mummies were made in Egypt for almost 4000 years. Mummy-makers experimented with different methods of preserving the dead, some of which worked better than others. The best mummies were made during a time of Egyptian history called the New Kingdom, between 3550 and 3069 years ago.

35 An ancient Greek called Herodotus wrote down one way the Egyptians made mummies. Herodotus visited Egypt in the 400s BC. He was told that it took 70 days to make a mummy – 15 days to cleanse the body, 40 days to dry it out and 15 days to wrap it.

36 Mummy-makers worked in open-air tents. Their simple workshops, which were far from villages and towns, were along the west bank of the river Nile. The tents were left open so that bad smells were carried away on the breeze. They were near the river as water was needed in the mummy-making process.

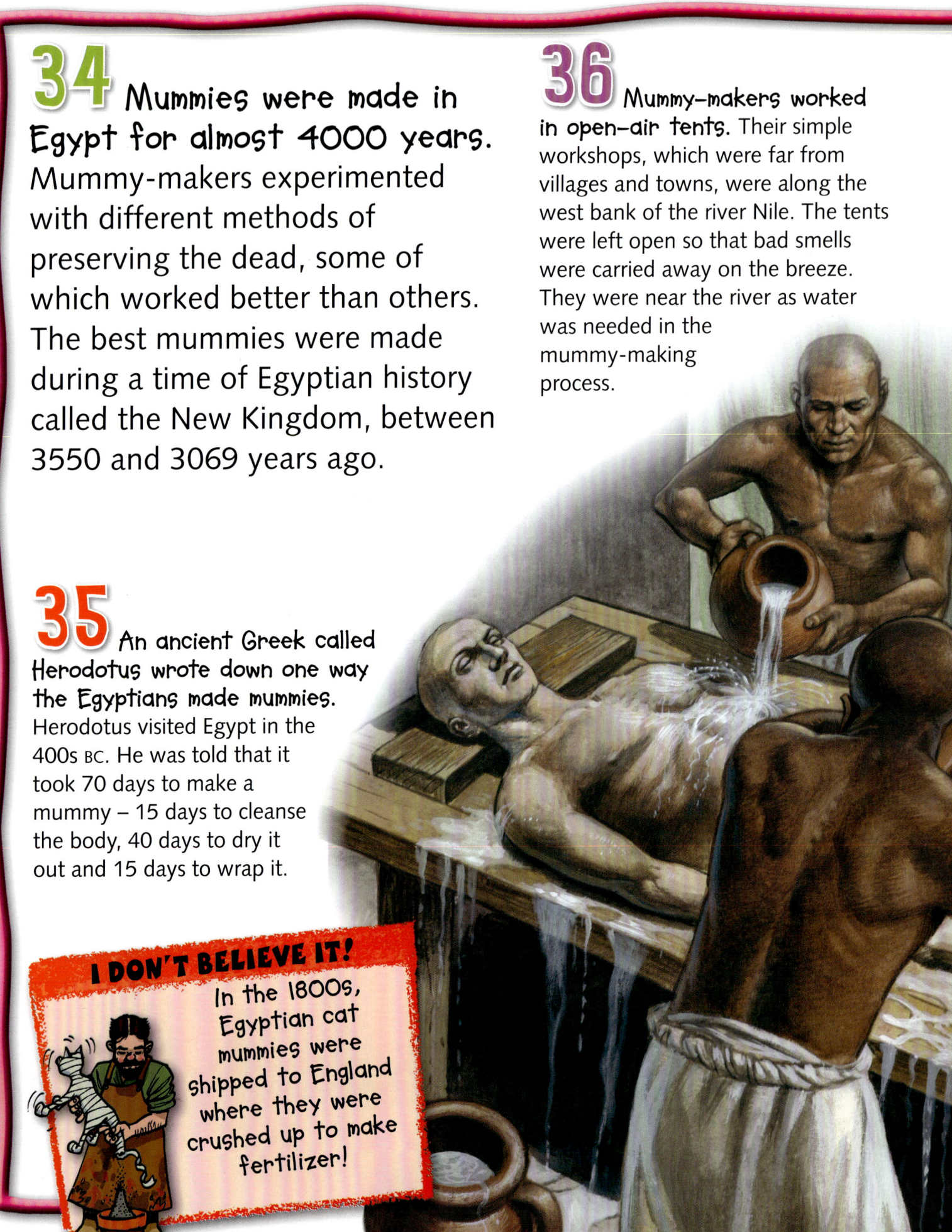

I DON'T BELIEVE IT!
In the 1800s, Egyptian cat mummies were shipped to England where they were crushed up to make fertilizer!

▶ To remove the brain, a metal hook was pushed up through the left nostril. It was then used to pull the brain out through the nose.

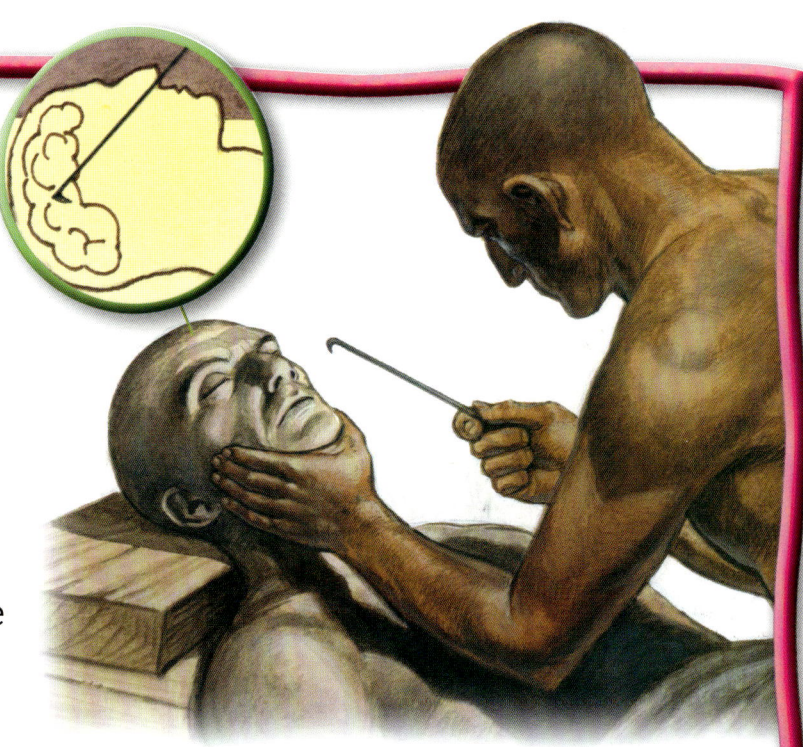

37 **Mummy-making skills were handed down from one generation to the next.** It was a job for men only, and it was a father's duty to train his son. A boy learned by watching his father at work. If his father worked as a slitter – the man who made the first cut in the body – his son also became a slitter.

38 **The first 15 days of making a mummy involved cleaning the body.** In the Place of Purification tent, the body was washed with salty water. It was then taken to the House of Beauty tent. Here, the brain was removed and thrown away. Then a slit was made in the left side of the body and the liver, lungs, intestines and stomach were taken out and kept.

39 **The heart was left inside the body.** The Egyptians thought the heart was the centre of intelligence. They believed it was needed to guide the person in the next life. If the heart was removed by mistake, it was put back inside. The kidneys were also left inside the body.

◀ A dead body was carefully washed with salty water before its organs were removed.

Drying the body

40 After the insides had been taken out, the body was dried. Mummy-makers used a special salt called natron to do the drying. The salt was a powdery-white mixture and was found along the edges of lakes in the north of Egypt. The natron was put into baskets, then taken to the mummy-makers.

41 At the workshop, small linen bags were filled with natron. The bags were packed into the empty body through the slit where the insides had been taken out. As well as the natron, rags, straw, dried grass and sawdust were also stuffed into the body. They helped to give the body its human shape.

▲ Some of the materials used by mummy-makers to stuff the bodies of mummies.

42 Next, the body was placed on its back on a table and covered in a thick layer of natron. No flesh was left exposed. The body was left to dry out under the natron for 40 days.

43 The liver, lungs, intestines and stomach were also dried. Each of these organs was placed in a separate pottery bowl, and natron was piled on top. Just like the body, these organs were also left for 40 days, during which time the natron dried them out.

44 Fishermen first used natron to dry the fish they caught. They realized that natron's salty crystals sucked juices out of dead flesh, leaving it dry. Dried, or salted, fish did not rot. This was why the mummy-makers began to use natron to preserve the dead.

45 During the 40 days of drying, the natron absorbed the body's juices. At the end of this time, the mummy-makers scraped away the natron and removed the materials used to stuff the body. The dried body had lost about three-quarters of its original weight and was shrivelled, hard and blue-black in colour. It hardly looked like a body at all.

▲ The body was covered in natron, a kind of salt, to dry it out. Up to 225 kilograms were needed.

Wrapped from head to toe

46 **The next job was to make the body appear lifelike.** The body cavity was filled and the skin was rubbed with oil and spices to make it soft and sweet-smelling. Then it was given false eyes and a wig, and make-up was applied. Lastly, tree resin was poured over it. This set into a hard layer to stop mould growing.

48 **The cut on the left side of the body was rarely stitched up.** Instead, it was covered with a wax plaque. On the plaque was a design known as the Eye of Horus. The Egyptians believed it had the power to see evil and stop it from entering the body through the cut.

47 **The dried-out organs were wrapped in linen, then put into containers called canopic jars.** The container with the baboon head (the god Hapi) held the lungs, and the stomach was put into the jackal-headed jar (the god Duamutef). The human-headed jar (the god Imseti) protected the liver, and the intestines were placed in the falcon-headed jar (the god Qebehsenuef).

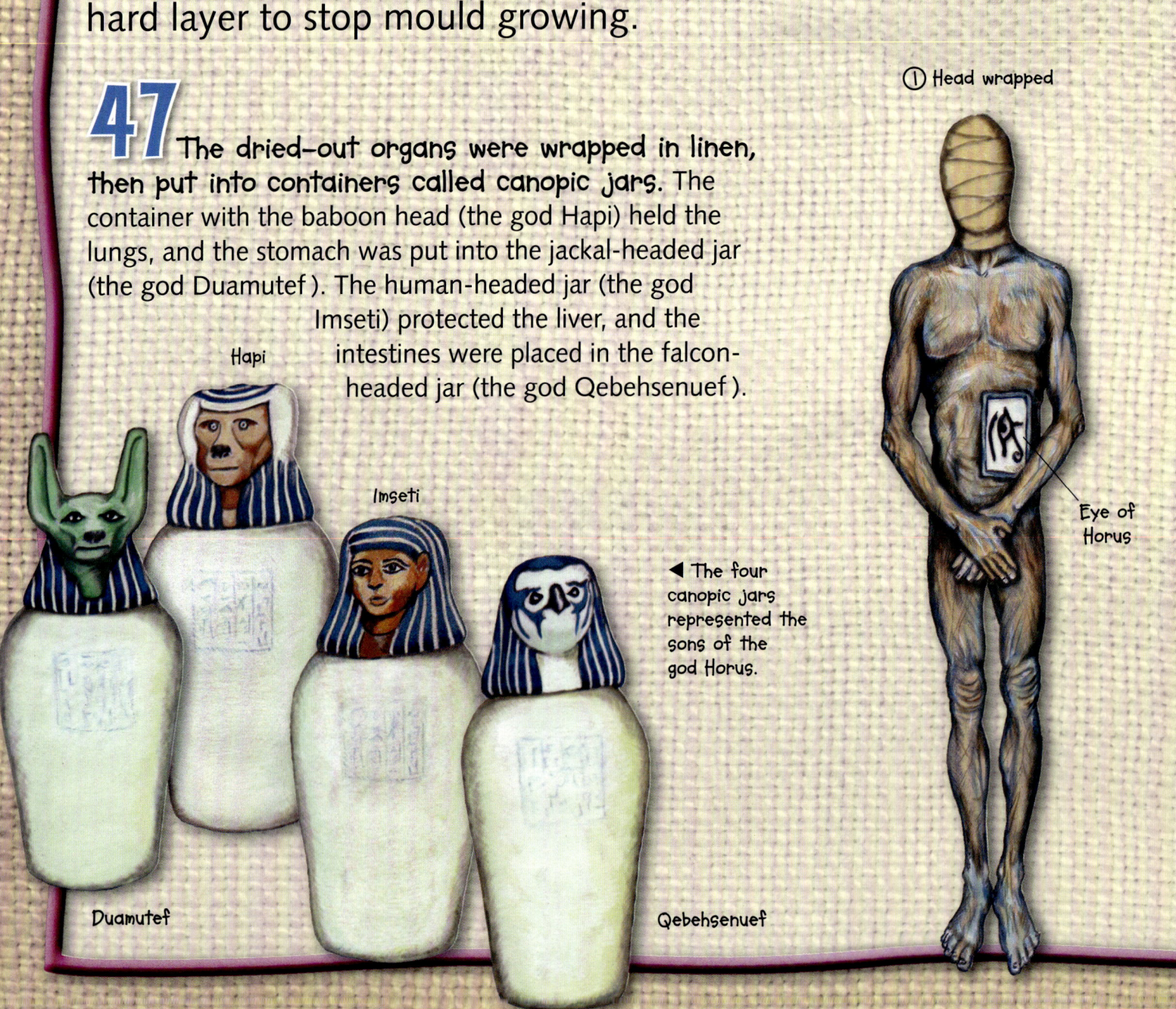

① Head wrapped

Eye of Horus

Hapi

Imseti

Duamutef

Qebehsenuef

◀ The four canopic jars represented the sons of the god Horus.

49 **In the final part of the process, the body was wrapped.** It took 11 days to do this. The body was wrapped in strips of linen, 6 to 20 centimetres wide. There was a set way of wrapping the body, which always started with the head. Lastly, the body was covered with a sheet of linen, tied with linen bands.

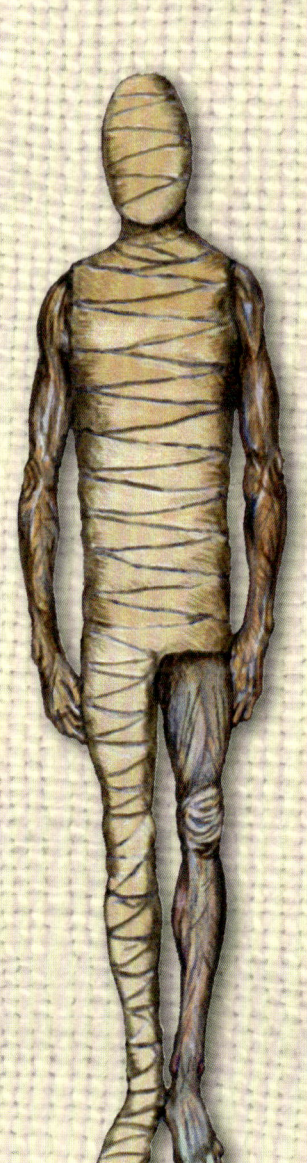

② Limbs and torso wrapped

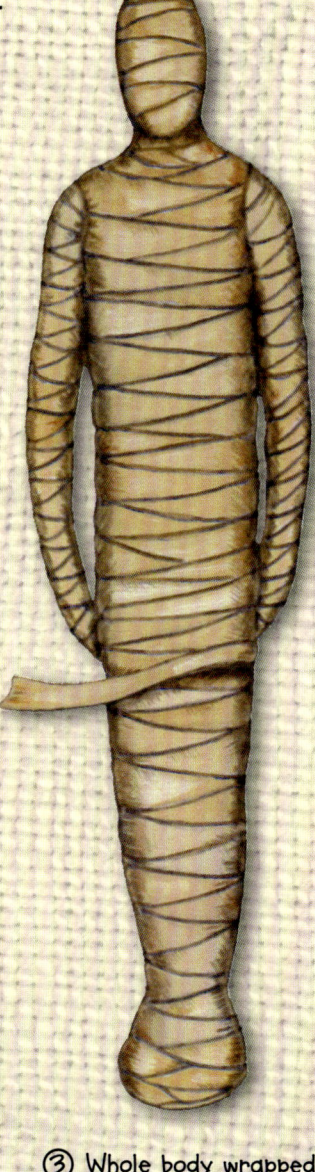

③ Whole body wrapped

▲ There was a five-stage sequence for wrapping the body, which always started with the head.

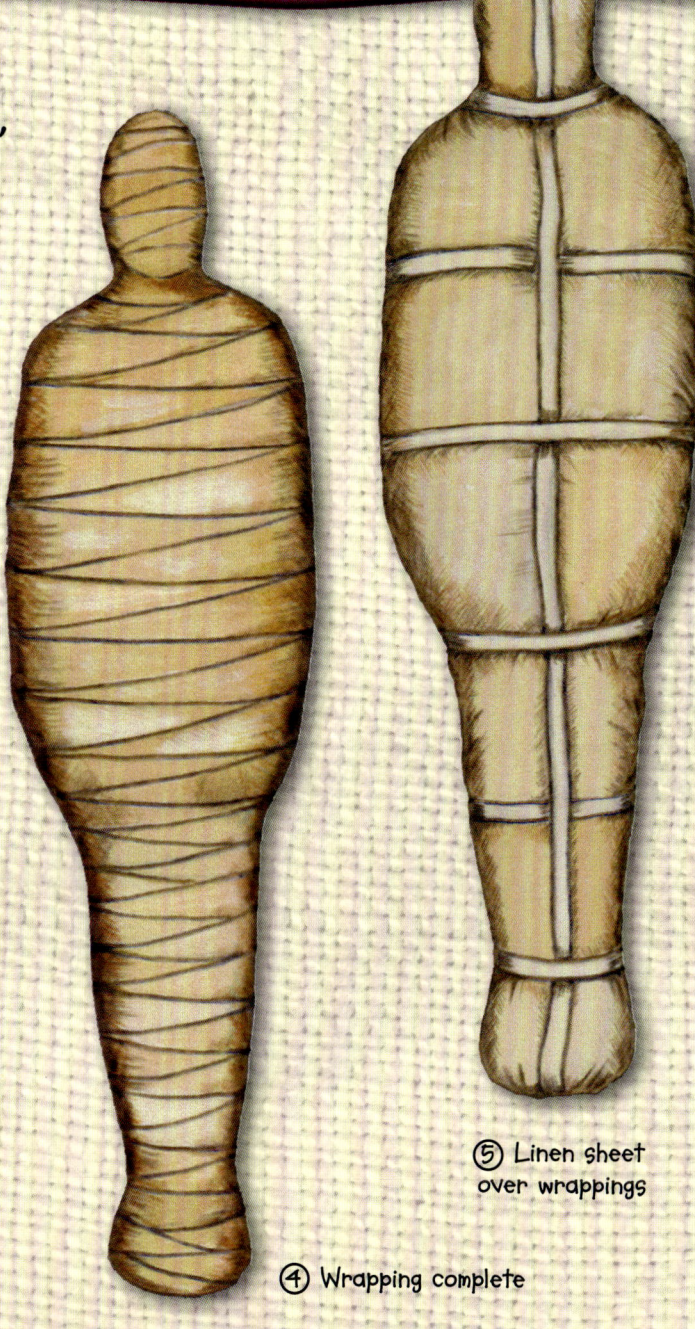

④ Wrapping complete

⑤ Linen sheet over wrappings

50 **During the wrapping, amulets (lucky charms) were placed between the layers of linen.** These protected the person from harm on their journey to the afterlife. Magic spells written on the wrappings were another form of protection. After it was wrapped, resin was poured over the mummy to make it waterproof. Last of all, it was given a face mask.

Tombs and tomb robbers

51 **The body was placed in a wooden coffin.** Simple coffins were made from planks of wood, and expensive ones were shaped like a person. They were decorated with spells. A picture on the inside of the coffin showed the route to the afterlife.

52 **The earliest pharaohs (kings) were buried in pyramid tombs.** The first pyramid was built about 2650 BC, for Pharaoh Djoser. For the next 800 years, all pharaohs were buried in pyramids. However, robbers found their way into all of them. Later pharaohs were buried in tombs cut into a rocky valley, known as the Valley of the Kings. Robbers found many of these tombs too, but not all.

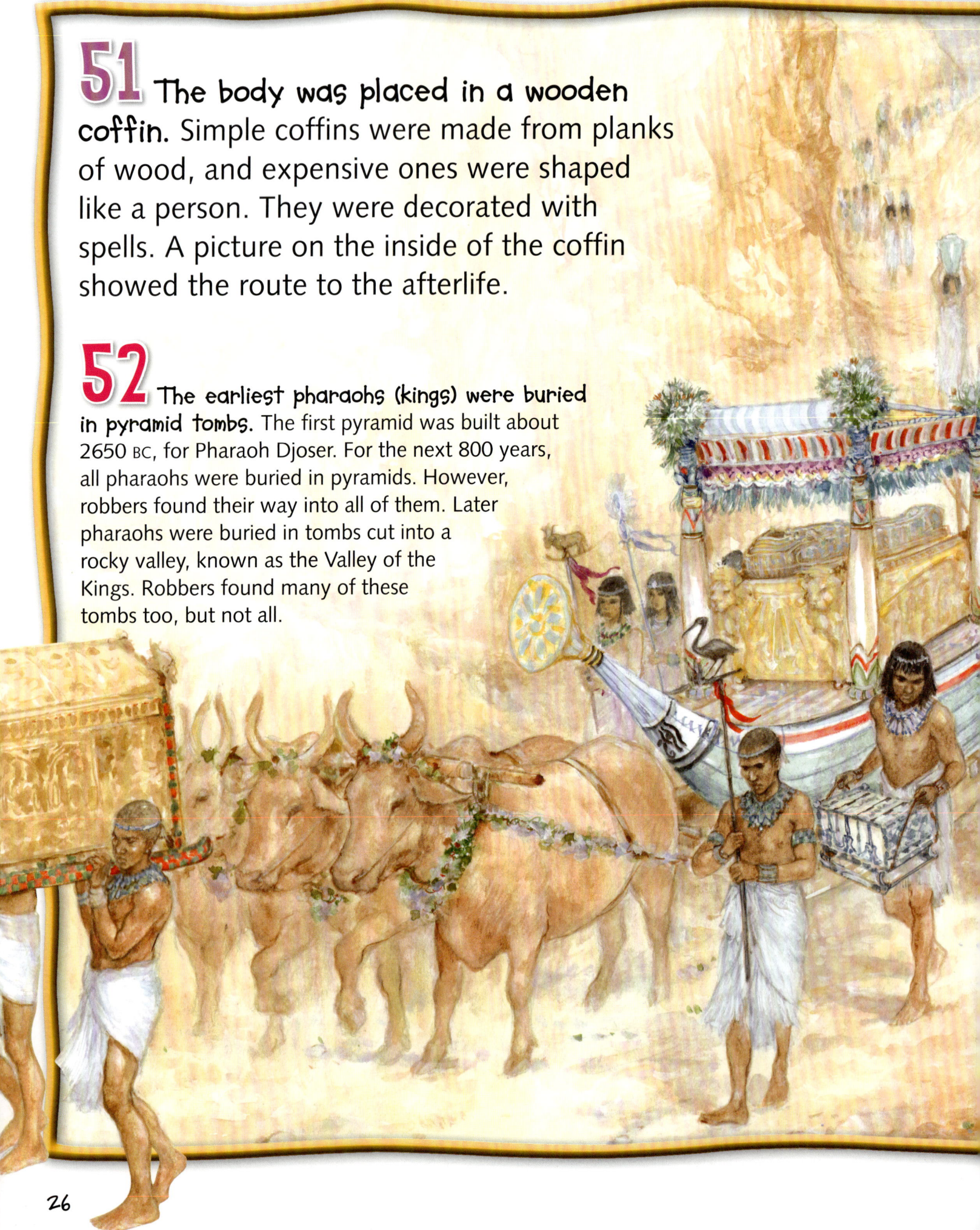

53 On the day of burial, the mummy was lifted out of its coffin and stood upright. A priest used a Y-shaped stone tool to touch the mummy's mouth, eyes, nose and ears. This was the Opening of the Mouth ceremony. It was done so that the person's speech, sight, hearing and smell came back to them for use in the next life.

▲ A priest (right) about to touch a mummy (left) in the Opening of the Mouth ceremony.

54 Mummies were buried with grave goods. These were items for the person to use in the next life. Ordinary people were buried with basic items, such as food and drink. Pharaohs and wealthy people were buried with everything they would need in their next life, such as furniture, clothes, weapons, jewellery and musical instruments.

55 Tombs were tempting places to robbers. They knew what was inside them, and took great risks to break in and steal the goods. Not even a mummy was safe – the tomb robbers smashed coffins open, and cut their way through the layers of linen wrappings to get at the masks, amulets and jewellery. Tomb robbery was a major crime, and if a robber was caught he was put to death.

◄ A funeral procession on its way to the Valley of the Kings. Oxen pulled the coffin on a wooden sledge shaped like a boat. This represented the deceased's journey to the next life.

Tutankhamun, the boy-king

56 Tutankhamun is one of Egypt's most famous pharaohs. He became king in 1334 BC when he was eight years old. Because he was too young to carry out the important work of ruling Egypt, two of his ministers took charge. They were Ay, chief minister, and Horemheb, head of the army. They made decisions on Tutankhamun's behalf.

▲ This model of Tutankhamun was buried with him in his tomb.

57 Tutankhamun was pharaoh for about nine years. He died when he was 17 years old. His body was mummified and buried in a tomb cut into the side of a valley. Many pharaohs were laid to rest in this valley, known as the Valley of the Kings. Tutankhamun was buried with valuables for use in the next life.

58 The tombs in the Valley of the Kings were meant to be secret. However, robbers found them, and stole the precious items buried there. They found Tutankhamun's tomb, but were caught before they could do much damage. Years later, when the tomb of Rameses VI was being dug, rubble rolled down the valley and blocked the entrance to Tutankhamun's tomb. After that, it was forgotten about.

59 In 1922, British archaeologist Howard Carter discovered the tomb of Tutankhamun. He had spent years searching for it. Other archaeologists thought he was wasting his time. They said all the tombs in the valley had already been found. Carter refused to give up, and in November 1922 he found a stairway that led to the door of a tomb.

◀ Found covering the head and shoulders of Tutankhamun's mummy, this beautiful mask features a royal cobra and a vulture's head, representing the unification of Upper and Lower Egypt.

▲ Tutankhamun's throne. The back is decorated with a picture of the pharaoh, who is seated, and a princess.

60 Behind the door was a corridor. At the end of it was a second door, which Carter made a hole in. He peered through the hole, and said he could see 'wonderful things'. It took ten years to remove all the objects from the tomb – jewellery and a gold throne were among the treasures. A gold mask covered the king's head and shoulders. It was made of 10 kilograms of pure gold.

Magnificent mummies!

61 **The mummy of pharaoh Ramses II was found in 1871.** It had been buried in a tomb, but had been moved to prevent robbers finding it. Ramses II had bad teeth, probably caused by eating gritty bread. He was in his eighties when he died and had arthritis, which would have given him painful joints. In 1976 his mummy was sent to France for treatment to stop mould from damaging it.

62 **Mummy 1770 is in the Manchester Museum, in the UK.** This is a mummy of a teenage girl, whose real name is not known. Her lower legs and feet are missing, and the mummy-makers had given her false ones to make her appear whole. It's a mystery what happened to her, but she might have been bitten by a crocodile, or even a hippo, as she paddled in the river Nile 3000 years ago.

▼ The mummy of Ramses II. Scientific studies have shown that particularly fine linen was used to stuff and bandage the body.

63 **A trapped donkey led to the discovery of thousands of mummies!** It happened in 1996, when a donkey slipped into a hole at Egypt's Bahariya Oasis. The owner freed it, then climbed down into an underground system of chambers lined with thousands of mummies of ordinary people. The site is called the Valley of the Golden Mummies, as many of the mummies have golden masks over their faces. They are about 2000 years old.

64 **Djedmaatesankh – Djed for short – is an Egyptian mummy in the Royal Ontario Museum, Toronto, Canada.** She lived around 850 BC, and in 1977 she entered the history books as the first Egyptian mummy to have a whole-body CAT scan (computerized axial tomography). The CAT images revealed that Djed had a serious infection in her jaw, which may have caused her death.

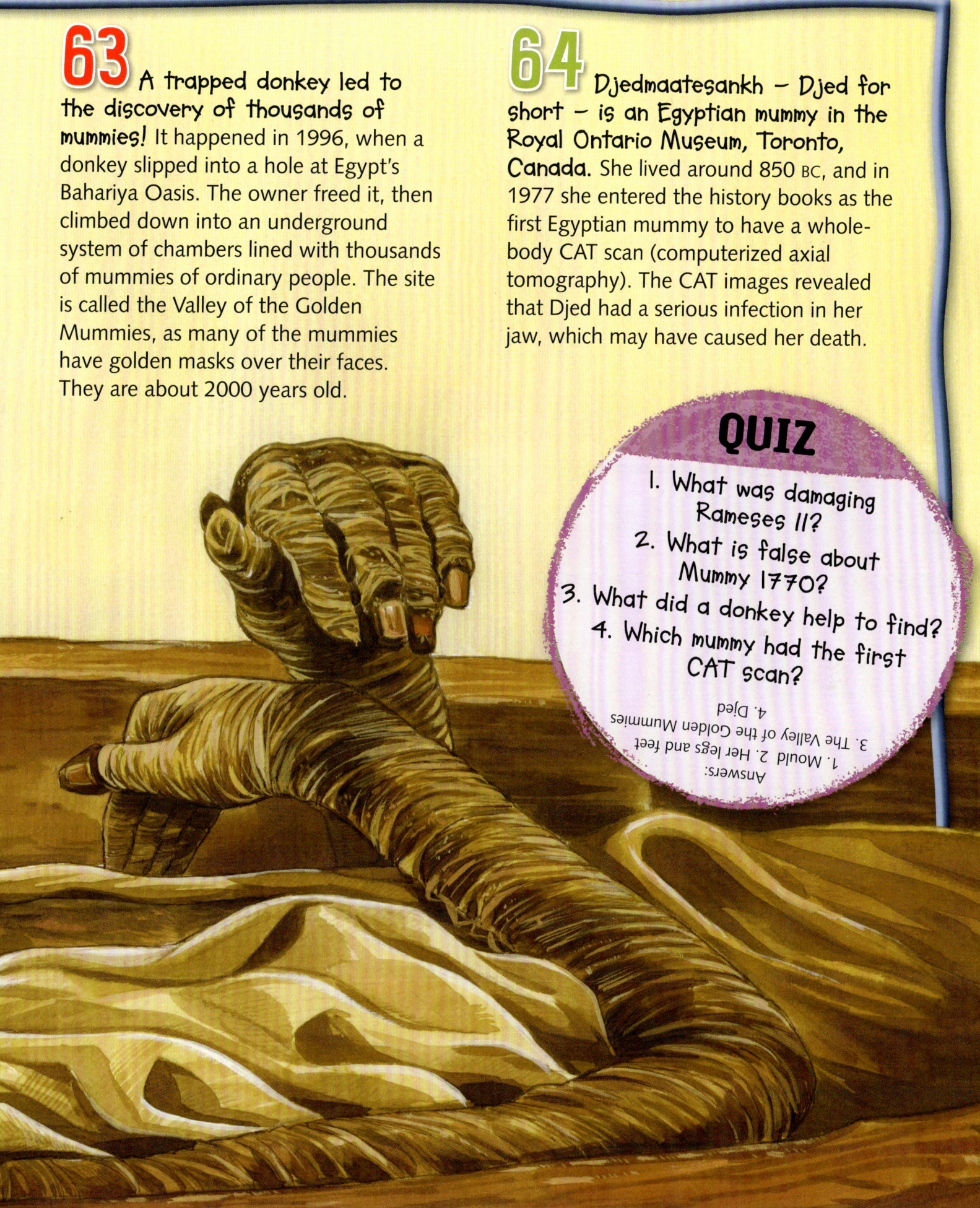

QUIZ

1. What was damaging Rameses II?
2. What is false about Mummy 1770?
3. What did a donkey help to find?
4. Which mummy had the first CAT scan?

Answers:
1. Mould 2. Her legs and feet 3. The Valley of the Golden Mummies 4. Djed

31

Mummies of Peru

65 Mummies were made in Peru, South America, for hundreds of years. The first were made in the 400s BC, and the last probably in the early 1500s. A body was put into a sitting position, with its knees tucked under its chin. Layers of cloth were wrapped around it to make a 'mummy bundle'. The body was preserved by the dry, cold environment.

▲ This mummy from Peru is more than 500 years old. It was covered in cloth to make a 'mummy bundle'.

66 In the 1500s, the mummies of Inca emperors were paraded through the streets of Cuzco, Peru. People thought that by doing this the souls of the dead were well-cared for, and this helped them on their journey into the afterlife. People also believed that this practice pleased the gods, who then ensured that living people were healthy and happy.

▲ Mummies of emperors were carried through the streets and put on display to the public.

I DON'T BELIEVE IT!

When Spaniards came to Peru in the 1500s, they destroyed thousands of Inca mummies — they got rid of 1365 in just four years!

67 **The Incas sacrificed children to their gods.** They hoped that in return the gods would provide rain for crops, good health and prosperity. The children's bodies were left at the tops of freezing mountains, where they slowly turned into natural mummies.

68 **In 1995, the mummy of a teenage Inca girl was found.** She was led to her death 500 years ago, as a sacrifice to the gods. Her body was left 6300 metres up Mount Ampato, Peru, with offerings of cloth, food, gold and silver. The icy conditions preserved her body.

▶ Inca children stand in front of a priest as they prepare to be sacrificed to the gods in a religious ceremony.

Mummies from Asia

69 More than 2500 years ago, the Pazyryk people of Siberia, Russia, buried their leaders in the region's frozen ground. In 1993, a Pazyryk burial mound was dug up, and inside was the frozen mummy of the 'Ice Princess'. She was dressed in clothes made from silk and wool, and she wore a pair of riding boots. When her body thawed from the ice, pictures of deer were found tattooed on her skin.

▲ The Pazyryk people tattooed images of snow leopards, eagles and reindeer onto their bodies. Those found on the 'Ice Princess' may have been a mark of her importance, or rank.

70 Lady Ch'eng is one of the world's best-preserved mummies. She was found in China, and is 2100 years old. Her body had been placed inside a coffin filled with a strange liquid that contained mercury (a silvery liquid metal, also known as quicksilver). The coffin was sealed and placed inside another, and then another. The coffins were buried under a mound of charcoal and clay, and in this watertight, airtight tomb, her body was preserved.

◄ This artist's impression shows how Lady Ch'eng may have looked when she was alive more than 2000 years ago.

QUIZ

1. What country did Vu Khac Minh come from?
2. What metal was in Lady Ch'eng's coffin?
3. What was on the skin of the Ice Princess?
4. How old are the Taklamakan mummies?

Answers:
1. Vietnam 2. Mercury 3. Tattoos 4. 3000 years

71 **Mummies have been found in China's Taklamakan Desert.** It hardly rains here, and the salty sand means that human bodies do not rot. It was a surprise when mummies were found in this remote place. They are about 3000 years old, and look Indo-European, not Chinese. It seems that long ago, a group of tall, light-skinned people settled in the east, where they died and were buried.

72 **Vu Khac Minh was a Buddhist monk from Vietnam.** In 1639, when he was near the end of his life, he locked himself in his room. He told his fellow monks to leave him alone for 100 days while he meditated (prayed). When this time was up, the monks found that he had died. His body was perfectly preserved and was put on view for all to see.

◀ Cherchen Man was just one of the many mummies found in the Taklamakan Desert.

North American mummies

73 **At 9000 years old, Spirit Cave Man is one of the oldest mummies.** The mummy was found in Spirit Cave, Nevada, USA, in 1940. It was wearing a cloak of animal skins, leather moccasins on its feet, and was wrapped inside mats made of tough grass. The cool, dry air in the cave had dried the body, turning it into a natural mummy.

▲ The mummy of Spirit Cave Man. Although it was discovered in 1940, the mummy's actual age was not determined until 1994.

74 **The mummy of the North American Iceman no longer exists.** It was found in 1999, in Canada. The Iceman had died in the 1400s, and was preserved in a glacier. Native North Americans claimed that the man was their ancestor, so the mummy was handed to them. It was cremated, and the ashes buried near where the mummy had been found.

75 **A mummy family was found on Greenland in 1972.** The bodies of six Inuit women and two children had been placed on a rocky ledge, in about 1475. The cold conditions had preserved them, slowly freeze-drying their bodies.

▶ An Inuit mummy of a baby boy. He was killed so that he could stay with his mother in the afterlife.

I DON'T BELIEVE IT!

Hazel Farris, like Elmer McCurdy, was an American outlaw whose mummified body was put on show at funfairs.

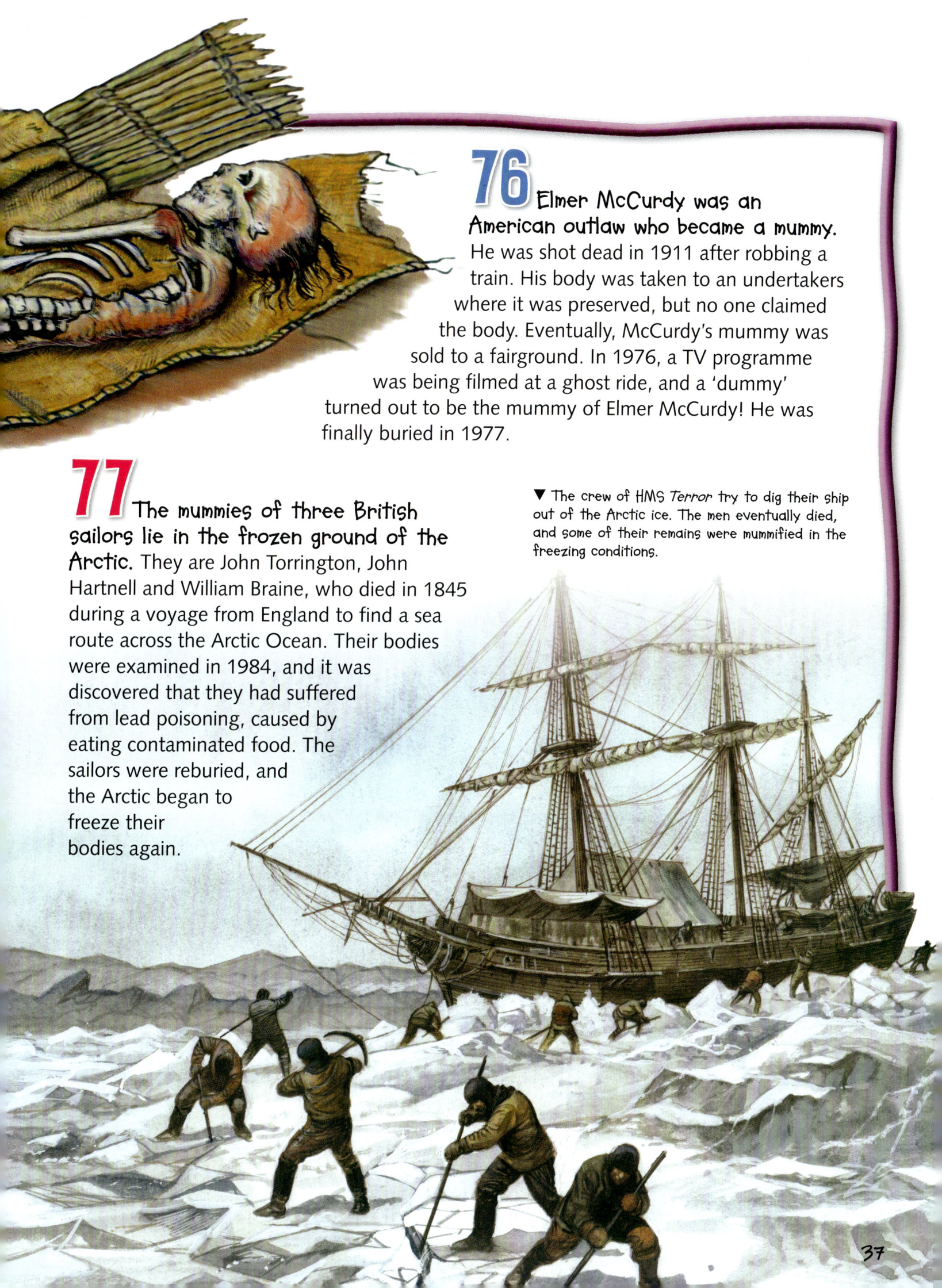

76 Elmer McCurdy was an American outlaw who became a mummy. He was shot dead in 1911 after robbing a train. His body was taken to an undertakers where it was preserved, but no one claimed the body. Eventually, McCurdy's mummy was sold to a fairground. In 1976, a TV programme was being filmed at a ghost ride, and a 'dummy' turned out to be the mummy of Elmer McCurdy! He was finally buried in 1977.

77 The mummies of three British sailors lie in the frozen ground of the Arctic. They are John Torrington, John Hartnell and William Braine, who died in 1845 during a voyage from England to find a sea route across the Arctic Ocean. Their bodies were examined in 1984, and it was discovered that they had suffered from lead poisoning, caused by eating contaminated food. The sailors were reburied, and the Arctic began to freeze their bodies again.

▼ The crew of HMS *Terror* try to dig their ship out of the Arctic ice. The men eventually died, and some of their remains were mummified in the freezing conditions.

Worldwide mummies

78 Mount Vesuvius is a volcano in southern Italy. It erupted in ad 79, and the town of Pompeii was buried under a layer of ash and rock. Many people died, mostly by suffocation. As scientists uncovered the town, they found body-shaped areas in the ground. By pouring plaster of Paris into the areas, the shapes of the dead were revealed.

▲ This plaster cast shows a victim of the Vesuvius eruption in AD 79. Some of the casts are so detailed, even facial expressions can be seen.

▼ Fully-dressed mummies line the walls of a church in Palermo, Italy. The dead wished to be preserved wearing their finest clothes.

79 In the underground crypt of a church in Palermo, Sicily, are more than 2000 human mummies. These are the bodies of local people, who were buried in the crypt more than 100 years ago. Instead of rotting away, the dry air has mummified their remains. Many of the mummies are propped against the walls, where they stand at odd angles, dressed in burial clothes.

80 The mummies of saints are displayed in many Roman Catholic churches. It isn't always the whole body that is on show, sometimes it is just a body part, called a 'relic'. Many of the mummies are natural, and are the result of being in a dry environment for many years. A few are artificial, and have been preserved on purpose. However, the Catholic Church believes that some saints have been preserved by God, and are evidence of miracles.

I DON'T BELIEVE IT!
The Guanche people of the Canary Islands, off the coast of West Africa, made mummies until the 1400s.

▲ The body of Saint Bernadette Soubirous (1844–1879) at Lourdes, France. Her body was exhumed (dug up) from her grave three times, and had not decomposed. People believed that she had been preserved by God.

81 Mummies have been made on the island of Papua New Guinea for generations. When a person died, they were put into a squatting position and their body was left to dry in the sun, or smoke-dried over a fire. Because the body was preserved, islanders believed their dead relatives were still living with them.

82 In Japan, there are about 20 mummies of Buddhist priests. The mummy of Tetsumonkai is one of them. He died in 1829, and a few years before his death he started to prepare his body for mummification. He ate less, and stopped eating rice, barley, wheat, beans and millet, as he believed that they harmed the body. After he died, his fellow priests put him in a sitting position with his legs crossed, and then dried out his body.

◀ The mummy of Tetsumonkai. His fellow priests dried his body by placing burning candles around it.

Studying mummies

83 Until recently, mummies were studied by opening them up. Unwrapping Egyptian mummies was popular in the 1800s, and was often done in front of an audience. Thomas Pettigrew (1791–1865) was an English surgeon who unwrapped many mummies at this time. He wrote some of the finest books about Egyptian mummies.

▲ An audience looks on as a mummy is unwrapped in the 1800s. This process destroyed lots of historical evidence.

84 There is no need to open up mummies today. Instead, mummies are studied by taking X-rays of bones, while scans reveal soft tissue in great detail. Mummies can even be tested to work out which families they came from.

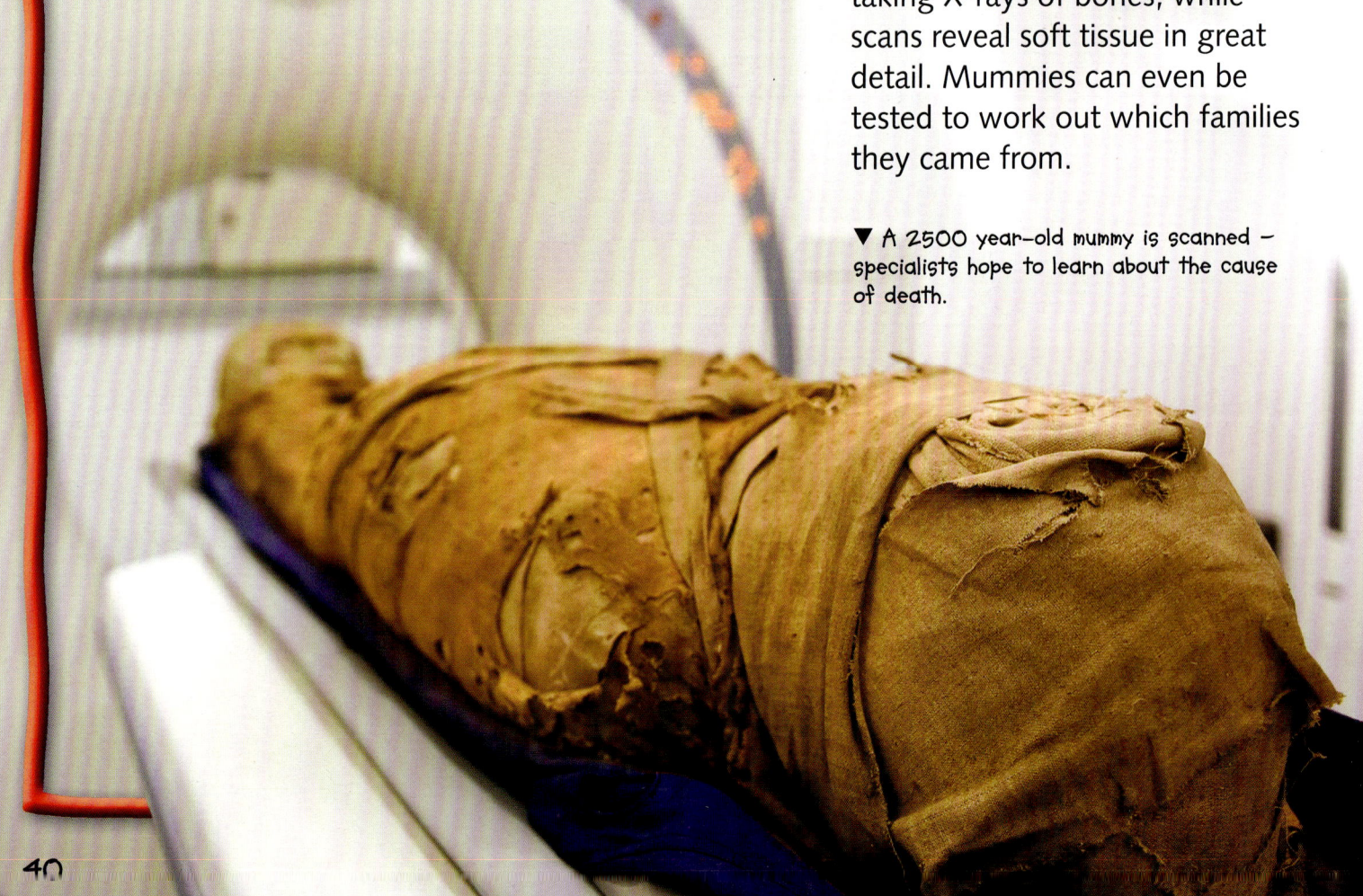

▼ A 2500 year-old mummy is scanned – specialists hope to learn about the cause of death.

▶ This X-ray of a mummy's skull reveals that a fractured skull was the cause of death.

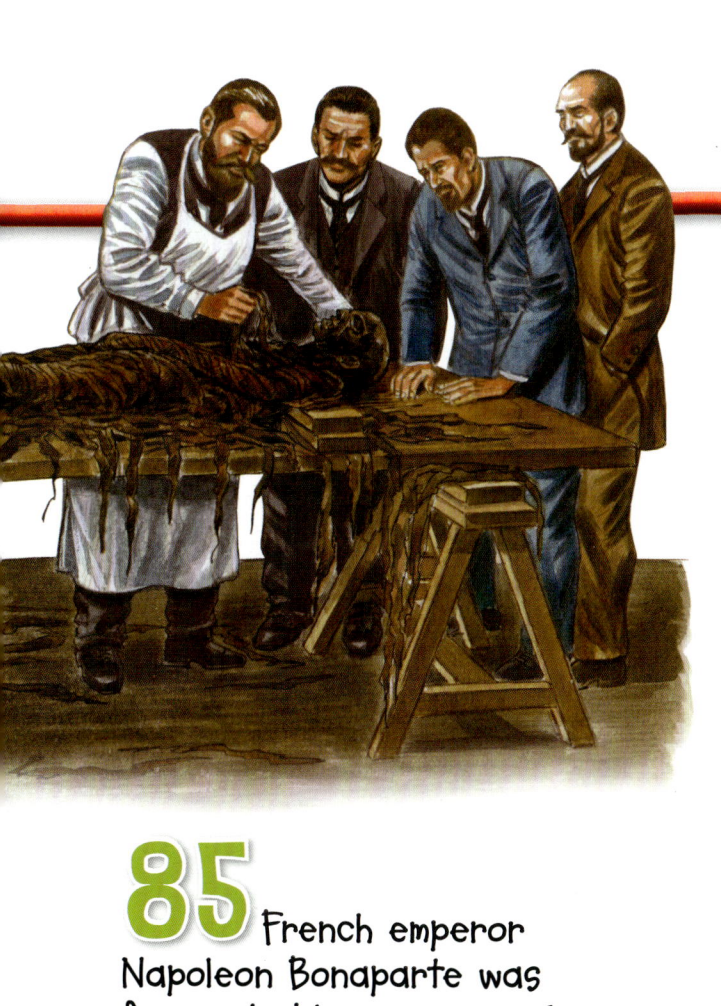

85 French emperor Napoleon Bonaparte was fascinated by mummies. After defeating the British in 1798, Napoleon and his troops became stranded in Egypt. With Napoleon were 150 scientists, who began to study Egypt and its mummies.

▼ When Napoleon left Egypt in 1799, he left behind a team of historians and scientists to study Egypt for him.

86 We can learn about the diseases and injuries people suffered by studying mummies. Egyptian mummies have been studied the most. We can tell they had problems with their health. Gritty bread damaged their teeth, parasites (worms) entered their bodies when they drank polluted water, insect bites caused fevers, and hard manual work led to problems with their joints and bones.

Animal mummies

87 Animals were mummified in ancient Egypt, too! Birds and fish were mummified as food for a dead person in the next life. Pet cats, dogs and monkeys became mummies so they could keep their dead owners company. Some bulls were believed to be holy as it was thought the spirits of the gods lived inside them. When they died, the bulls were mummified and buried in an underground tomb.

▲ Crocodiles were sacred to the Egyptian god Sobek. They were probably mummified in the same way as humans, then wrapped up.

▼ Fur is still visible around the feet of Dima, the baby mammoth.

88 A baby mammoth was found in the frozen ground of Siberia in 1977. Many of these ancient elephant-like animals have been found in this part of Russia. What made this one special was the near-perfect state of its body. The animal was about a year old when it died, and was named Dima, after a stream close to where it was discovered.

QUIZ

1. How old is Dima?
2. Which animal is linked to the goddess Bastet?
3. What did Charles Sternberg find?
4. Did the Egyptians mummify crocodiles?

Answers:
1. 40,000 years old 2. Cat
3. A mummy of a dinosaur 4. Yes

89 **The world's oldest mummy is a dinosaur.** It is the fossil of *Edmontosaurus*, which was found in Wyoming, USA, in 1908. This dinosaur died 65 million years ago, but instead of becoming a skeleton, its body was baked dry by the sun. When US fossil hunter Charles Sternberg discovered it, the skin and insides had been fossilized, as well as the bones.

▲ This frog was naturally mummified in 2006 when it died in a plant pot. The sun baked it dry.

90 **Cats have been made into mummies for thousands of years.** In ancient Egypt, cats were linked to the goddess, Bastet. They were bred to be killed as religious offerings at temples. Cat mummies are sometimes found behind the walls of old houses in Europe. It was believed a cat could bring good fortune, so a cat's body was sometimes walled up, after which it dried out until it was a natural mummy.

▲ This mummified cat was found in 1971 in Sudbury, Suffolk, UK. It had been walled up in an old mill to protect the building from harm.

Mummy stories

91 The idea of the 'mummy's curse' started in 1923. A letter printed by a London newspaper said people would be cursed if they disturbed any pharaoh's tomb. Tutankhamun's tomb had just been found and people seemed to believe in curses. The letter seemed to confirm their fears. In fact, the entire thing was all made up!

▼ The opening of Tutankhamun's tomb by Howard Carter was the basis for the 'curse of the mummy'.

92 Mummies have not been used to make newspaper! There's a story that says linen was stripped from the mummies of Egypt, then used to make paper. The story goes on to say that an American newspaper was printed on this so-called 'mummy paper', sometime in the 1800s. It's a great story, but it's not true!

93 A mummy didn't sink *Titanic* in 1912! In the British Museum, London, is the lid of an Egyptian coffin. It is known as the 'Unlucky Mummy' as it's thought to be cursed. English journalist William Stead was on board *Titanic* when it sank. He told a story about the 'Unlucky Mummy' on the night the ship sank, and some people believed that this cursed the voyage.

▼ The 2001 film *The Mummy Returns* used lots of creepy special effects.

▼ A scene from the 1932 film *The Mummy*. Boris Karloff played the part of the mummy character, Im–Ho–Tep (left).

94 Mummies have become film stars. The first mummy film was made in 1909 and was called *The Mummy of King Rameses*. It was a black-and-white film without any sound. Many mummy films have been made since. One of the creepiest was *The Mummy*. It was made in 1932, and starred Boris Karloff.

95 As long ago as 1827, a book was written about a mummy. *The Mummy! A Tale of the Twenty-second Century* was written by Jane Loudon. The book was a science fiction story set in the year 2126. Lots more stories have been written about mummies since then – some for children. The author Jacqueline Wilson has even written *The Cat Mummy*, about a girl who tries to mummify her dead cat!

QUIZ

1. Was there a mummy on board *Titanic*?
2. Which mummy film did Boris Karloff star in?
3. What started in 1923?
4. Who wrote *The Cat Mummy*?

Answers:
1. No 2. The Mummy 3. The mummy's curse 4. Jacqueline Wilson

Modern-day mummies

96 **In Moscow, Russia, and in Beijing, China, modern-day mummies can be found.** When Vladimir Ilich Lenin died in 1924, his body was mummified and put on display in Moscow. The same thing happened in China in 1976, when Mao Zedong died. Both men were leaders of their countries, and after they died, their bodies were preserved so that people could continue to see them.

▲ The mummy of Lenin is still on display in Moscow, Russia. The body was preserved using a secret technique.

97 **The wife of a leader was also mummified.** Eva Perón was the wife of the president of Argentina. After her death in 1952, her body was preserved. Then in 1955 the Argentine government was overthrown, and Eva's mummy was sent to Europe. It was returned to Argentina in 1974 to be buried.

I DON'T BELIEVE IT!

When the British artist Edward Burne-Jones found out that his paint was made from mummy remains, he buried the tube, and put daisies on the 'grave'!

98 **An old man was mummified in America in 1994.** A team of experts became the first people in modern times to mummify a human using ancient Egyptian techniques. They used the same tools as those used by the Egyptian mummy-makers. Then the organs were removed, the body was dried with natron and wrapped in linen.

99 **If you have $67,000 (about £52,000) to spare, you can have your dead body mummified!** Odd as it sounds, there's a company in America that will carry out an Egyptian-style mummification on people. It's cheaper to have a cat or a dog mummified, and the smaller the pet, the less it costs!

100 **Modern animal mummies have become works of art.** English artist Damien Hirst has taken dead animals such as sheep, cows and sharks and preserved them with a special chemical. They have then been displayed to the public in art galleries as works of art.

▼ This preserved sheep was put on display in London by Damien Hirst in 1994.

Index

Page numbers in **bold** refer to main subject entries.

A
afterlife 8, 16, 19, 25, 26, 27, 32
America 46, 47
Ampato, Mount 33
amulets 25, 27
animals 16, **42–43**, 47
Arctic Ocean 37
Argentina 46
Asia **34–35**

B
Bahariya Oasis 31
Bernadette, St 39
bitumen 6
bog bodies **12–13**, **14–15**
Burne-Jones, Edward 46

C
Canada 36
Canary Islands 39
canopic jars 24
Carter, Howard 7, 29, 44
Catholic Church 39
cats 20, 42, 43, 47
charms 25
Ch'eng, Lady 34
Cherchen Man 35
Chile 8–9
China 34, 35, 46
Chinchorro people **8–9**
cleaning the body **20–21**
coffins 17, 26, 27, 29, 34
crocodiles 42
curses 44
Cuzco 32

D
Denmark 12, 13
dinosaurs 43
Djedmaatesankh 31
Djoser, Pharaoh 26
drying the body **22–23**

E, F
embalming 16
Eye of Horus 24
films 45

G
Germany 13
glaciers 10
gods 19, 24, 32, 33
gold 29, 31, 33
Grauballe Man 13
grave goods 27
Greenland 36
Guanche people 39

H
Herodotus 20
Hirst, Damien 47

I
'Ice Princess' 34
Iceman **10–11**, 36
Incas **32–33**
Inuit 36
Isis 18–19
Italy 10–11, 38

J, K
Japan 39
jewellery 27, 29
Karloff, Boris 45

L
Lenin, Vladimir Ilyich 46
Lindow Man **14–15**
linen 24, 25, 27, 30, 44, 46

M
mammoths 42
Mao Zedong 46
masks 8, 25, 27, 29, 31
McCurdy, Elmer 37
'mummy bundles' 32
Mummy 1770 30
myths **18–19**

N
Napoleon I, Emperor 41
natron 22–23, 46
North America **36–37**

O
Opening of the Mouth 27
organs 21, 22, 24, 46
Osiris **18–19**

P
Palermo 38
Papua New Guinea 39
Pazyryk people 34
peat bogs **12–13**, **14–15**
Perón, Eva 46
Peru **32–33**
Pettigrew, Thomas 40
pharaohs 7, 16, 26, 27, **28–29**, 44
plaques 24
Pompeii 38
pyramids 26

R
Rameses II, Pharaoh 30–31
Rameses VI, Pharaoh 28
relics 39
resin 24, 25
robbers 17, 26, 27, 28, 30
Russia 42, 46

S
sacrifices 15, 33
salt **22–23**
sand 16, 35
Seth **18–19**
Siberia 34, 42
Sicily 38
South America **8–9**, **32–33**
spells 25, 26
Spirit Cave Man 36
studying mummies **40–41**

T
Taklamakan Desert 35
Terror, HMS 37
Titanic 45
Tollund Man 12
tombs **26–27**, 44
Tutankhamun 6–7, **28–29**, 44

U, V
unwrapping mummies 40–41
Valley of the Golden Mummies 31
Valley of the Kings 26, 27, 28
Vesuvius, Mount 38
Vietnam 35
Vu Khac Minh 35

W, Y
Wilson, Jacqueline 45
Windeby Girl 13
wrapping the body **24–25**
Yde Girl 13